MW01595720

Transmissions

for

Humanity

Book I

**Guidance From Higher Dimensional
Beings During This Pivotal Time in
Human Evolution**

Copyright © 2020 by Vickie Verlie
-All rights reserved-

ISBN: 9798673372623

Contents

Introduction

Growing up near the shores of Lake Erie I've always loved going to the lake, it is a magical place. Some would write off the high vibes as negative ions. While that may be partially true, there is something more happening there. Perhaps something otherworldly, something beyond our comprehension.

I would often get message while relaxing at the lake, usually pertaining to whatever I was grappling with at the time. One cold winter's day in February of 2019 I decided to take a notebook and start taking dictation. What followed was series of messages and conversations with a group of earth spirits. As time progressed the communications evolved to include other higher dimension beings as well.

On the day of my first communication, I got a vision of very tall beings wading in the water. They were as tall as a building, and the lake water was only waste high. With the mean depth of Lake Erie being 62 feet deep, that would put their height at over 100 feet! The beings in this first encounter were long and lean and had a pointed head. Immediately I was reminded of the 1960s Japanese television show Ultraman.

The beings I saw were not metallic or robotic as with Ultraman, but rather smooth skinned and organic looking. Still the height and overall body type was very similar to the Ultraman character. Interestingly, I have been drawing pointy headed creatures since I was a child. Additionally I have seen art created by several local artists with the same signature pointy heads. Although none of the art was the same as the creatures wading in the lake, it can't be merely coincidence that we all brought forth this kindred imagery.

As I began communicating with them other imagery emerged, different "versions" of these very large beings. I now realize that they were reaching out to me and trying to communicate for quite some time, perhaps even my whole life.

Most notably in the fall of 2016 I saw a strange looking oil stain that looked like some sort of creature. After posting it on social media, a friend commented that it looked like the forest spirit from Princess Mononoke. At the time I had no idea what she was talking about. After googling it I found a pic that closely resembled my oil stain! I gave it no more thought at the time other than being a cool synchronicity.

Around that same time a strange looking deer ran in front of my car and into a back yard of a house. It caught my attention because I had never seen a deer quite like it before.

After doing a fair amount of research I concluded that it was a reindeer, and the message was that something was going to happen around Christmas. I knew at the time that is wasn't exactly like a reindeer, but that was the closest I could find. My logical mind was tired of looking for a match to what I saw, and a wonderful Christmas gift sounded good to me!

Once I began communing with these beings, I saw an image in my minds eye that was similar to the oil stain in the parking lot a few years before. This prompted me to investigated the Princess Mononoke story further.

It turns out that the Forest Spirit of the animated movie is based on the Japanese legend of the Daidarabotchi. This giant forest spirit was said to have created lakes with it's foot prints and takes the form of a deerlike animal! The synchronicity was uncanny and It all started to make sense now. I realized that the were reaching out to me since 2016! Now nearly three years later, I finally took pen to hand to convey their message.

As I opened up to the higher vibrations and my consciousness expanded, I began to get messages from other higher dimensional beings as well.

During the course of these sessions sometimes they would just start talking, and other times I would ask questions. Sometimes the questions were about what was going on in my life at the time.

Although their wisdom helped me see things from a higher perspective, I have omitted the majority of those transmissions because of personal details involved. Some still remain because I felt they may have value to others on their journey.

The channeled information is in plain text, while my questions and comments are italicised. Their communications have been left virtually unedited as to not distort the original message.

February 18th 2019

First Transmission

Things are moving slowly now but will speed up substantially when the wind blows. We migrated here from other planets and are present most of your world's oceans.

Many more will begin to see us as we are entering into an accelerated time warp, as the shift has begun. It is not a violent all at once, though some places will seem like it, as natural disasters in the "normal" range are occurring worldwide.

Are mine and others physical symptoms due to the shifting energy?

Physical bodies are acclimating to the higher dimensions, as we are higher dimensional what you would call "beings." We are older than the Earth, as old as your Sun. We are caretakers, the watchers of your race and this planet's sentient beings. We are moving energy, the water receives energy from us, and we from it. Transmuting toxins and replenishing the environment. We turn toxins into energy.

Tell us more about your race.

We lived in a lush planet billions of years ago and ventured out to other worlds. Very lush, green and purple moss, a damp moist environment.

We have no voice, we communicate with higher tones like music, musical waves of energy. Lush and beautiful. There is a thick atmosphere and we move slowly through the thick moist air, not unlike the Avatar movie.

Like the Sea monkey cartoons in the back of comic books?

Yes many people tune in and pick up on us to some extent. Also the Outer Limits and others. But they added their own fear to make us seem like monsters.

Do you live here?

Some of the time, but in another dimension, not in your 3D reality. Dolphins - they are our friends. They are very aware of us as they are also multidimensional creatures. They are one of our animal companions, like your dogs would be to you.

What do you eat?

We don't eat, but charge through the energy of the water. There are different tribes all over your earth that have evolved over time.

Redwood Forest, Rain forest.. these different
tribes are offshoots of our family, like cousins.
We have evolved to be more aquatic, while
others are more connected to the Earth.

Like the Fairy or Devic Creatures?

No, but we communicate with them as well.
Like the dolphins, they are aware of us and
we are aware of them.

There are countless forms of terrestrial beings
that reside in the Earth plane, and travel in and
out of this planetary system. Most of mankind are
unaware of our presence, others would like to
believe we are omnipresent. Some want to believe
that they are in control of everything, that they
are the most powerful, when there are myriads
of other possibilities.

What about the giant geode?
(Lake Erie is home to the largest Geode in
the world)

It is an energy source for the lake area. It vibrates
or breathes, but it is at a rate that is undetectable
to humans. It is a living breathing organism for lack
of a better term. It is also a guidance system of
some sort, so that interdimensional travelers may
find their way.

March 28th 2019

Listen...hear the heartbeat of the land. There
is a rhythm in all things.

April 23rd 2019

Earth Guardians

New time line, the beginning and the end, the
end and the beginning. Cycles of time, cycles of
war, cycles of dream, cycles of life. We are with
you all the time not only when you come here
(the lake) we join you on your video transmissions,
we fly with you in your dreams.

There is a peace that can be found in the stillness
of your heart. We are the listeners, the guides, the
guardians, the ancient ones (birds calling/chirping)

We speak through the ocean, the land, the air, the
sea. All of nature is aware of our presence except
the humans. Humans are so busy with their lives
in acquiring, aspirin, achieving, but not taking
time just to be. Observe instead of force, receive
instead of push. Understand that all force is
working together in harmony with the great
creator spirit. Believe and all things will appear.

We are going through a great transition of spirit and consciousness. Many are awakening, yet many are still in sleep.

I had to move to another spot due to noise.

Yes the noise can be disruptive to receiving our signal. Those who perpetuate it are unaware of their involvement. When a light is bright it draws the opposite. This is an environment of polarity. Your light can still shine, it can be achieved.
A change is coming for you of great importance.
It will allow you to grow in spirit and continue your work of raising consciousness to the masses in this great awakening.

What can I do about the mental chatter?

Clear your mind and start again. The advice you give others is also for you. When you channel it is clear and is easier to raise your vibration along with the holy spirit.

The sea and the wind are fluid, and carry kinetic energy that seeps into the very essence of your being. Energy that has been trapped in the physical body can be dislodged, transmuted and swept away in a very natural way, restoring harmony and balance.

We are as old as the Earth and we were assigned as her guardians or stewards eons ago.

It is not been that long from our perspective as we are moving in a different time space than you. That is why when we do our sessions with you time seems very different. You are brushing up against another realization of time.

time would behave differently when I was at the lake channeling. Usually it would fly by. I would think I was writing for maybe 15 minutes, when really a couple of hours had gone by.

June 18th 2019

Affirmations

Feel the breeze that whispers to you and transports you to another time. Altering your perception of this perceived reality. The dust flies from the sky bringing messages, too many to catch from the great beyond. From those who came before, and those yet to be in this time. Ripples in the water. Rippling waves of consciousness coming in, receiving all the time. May this day bring you peace and contentment as you navigate the sometimes turbulent waters of this space.

Affirmation - peace, release, peace, release, peace, release... On and on, never ending. Rejuvenating, glowing, showing, knowing.

Ideas taking shape in your mind, in your reality, constantly realizing. Pick a stream and ride in it.

September 4th 2019

Earth Reviving

The truth must be told, things are about to unfold.
Unfold like an origami of infinite detail. The
details are wide and far reaching, exposing many
to the great waves of consciousness that are
coming through at this time of unfolding that is
taking place now. The great shifts are occurring
in this world as well as others. We are all
interconnected in infinite multiverses of time
and space. One thing cannot change without
affecting the other. For every action there is an
equal opposite reaction emphasis on "re."

We are transmitting the golden nuggets of the era.
The transformational tools needed for the massive
waves of consciousness that is coming through.
Unlock the door to other dimensional realities
that coexist in the Multiverse. Seasons change
and the Earth revives and renews herself.
The great journey of discovery is this time of
acceleration like man has not seen before on this
planet. There were attempts in the past, but the
energy of fear was too strong to allow the force to
be fully realized.

It seems that way now.

It is a great purging of the last remnants of a bygone era on Earth.

The birth of the Golden Dawn is upon us. Stand up and say your peace. There are many feeling this way and looking for connection. There is strength in numbers my dear. It's time to speak out and hold your truth dear.

For you are a pioneer of thought, and thoughts become actions. There are millions of starseeds descending on this planet, and the momentum grows stronger all the time.

Like trying to move a giant boulder, or a car stuck in the snow. More and more come to help push, and not lose momentum. Until we finally roll from forward, and the momentum accelerates our spiritual growth and advancement. For you see we shall advance too, as will others not in the flesh at this time.

(Caterpillar crawling up my leg)

It is a joint effort between many on different planes of existence. Those in the flesh, in spirit, then us. Many levels are expanding on this giant push to give birth to this new era. Emergence - facilitate the emergence of higher dimensional frequencies.

October 2nd 2019

Seasons Change

The end of the season is drawing near. Not only the year, but of the bigger time or epoch. The epoch of the time of Christ, epoch of growth and suffering.

As the music comes to your ears, so do the shifting times. Shifting from one age to another, the eternal cycle of life.

This planet is moving, ascending. The oceans are moving in a fluid motion, guiding, caressing gently forward. There is a gathering of souls from all walks of life. From all stratospheres, all dimensions, all species, to be here for this monumental moment. The Earth is shedding her skin, to begin another great cycle into the new dimension. As we come aboard to give her a push, a boost. To propel her into the next step of evolution.

Music and tones, harmonies, open portals and gateways. Yes it is the time of the great listening, the great awakening. The great summit in the sky, and we are all invited to participate. Partake in the energetic release from this dimension.

The dogma that has kept humanity and chains for eons. We are lifting the veil, shedding our skins to bring fourth new multi-dimensional experiences in this journey of a lifetime!

October 21st 2019

Parallel Existence

As I'm waiting for the messages to come, I see a duck on the water.

The creatures of the sea can go their whole life without ever being aware of the world above. That has been the human condition for some time. Now many are coming to the surface and getting a glimpse of the world outside of this construct, outside of this dimension. There is a whole universe that is waiting for you to wake up and join the bigger reality that humanity is already a part of.

October 24th 2019

Consciousness Evolution

We are ready to begin the next level of consciousness evolution.

The lake is rough today. I noticed the waves crashing on the rocks.

The water crashes on the rocks, but we are safe and untouched on the solid ground. Although turbulence is all around we can still maintain our flow of higher energy, and need not engage in the distress. Rocking, bubbling from the Earth's surface, the turbulence of change is upon us.

The tide comes in and goes out, but always returns. There is no ending, no beginning.

What is the message for the masses?

Keep seeking, keep rising, keep growing, keep knowing, keep digging, keep singing, keep laughing, keep loving, keep flowing.

We are moving the Earth into a new dimension, a new season. Many will not be aware because their mind knows what it knows. Just as a natives of this land could not see the ships at sea, most of your scientists will not know the difference. They know what they know, and it is a FACT! Facts are undeniable, irrefutable, proven by scientific data. But still we ARE changing, whether they believe it or not.

Are the flat earthers challenging the known science?

Yes that is part of it, but the message is muddled or skewed. The Earth is contracting and morphing to get through this portal. Like a bouncing ball viewed in slow motion. You are unable to see it with your naked eye, but slowed down it is very clear to see the ball changing shape as it bounces.

Just as we told you of how time moves differently from our slower perspective. People talking about flat Earth are picking up on that on some level, but the message is horribly skewed. For the most part they are coming from an ego perspective and trying to maintain power or influence power over others. Most are very angry, and anger and aggression is of the ego not of the soul/spirit.

Yes the Earth's changing and morphine all the time. Like the bouncing ball or like an egg that gets sucked through a bottle in your science experiments. Humans on Earth cannot perceive it, although they do feel it sometimes. Your vertigo for example.

Are vertigo episodes jumping timelines?

We are always jumping timelines, and yes it is more prevalent now. But it is not exactly the way you are thinking of it. Humans are jumping timelines all the time, whether vertigo is present or not.

What about the forest spirit? Was that you in the oil stain?

Yes and yes. All parts of our family as was explained earlier.

We've been with you your whole life. The oil stain was the first time that you saw us clearly, or noticed us. You were doing a lot of readings again, and it does raise your consciousness, although we are aware that it drains you so.

That chapter of your journey is nearly complete, as we have direct contact now.

Good, I like this better than doing readings, it's low vibes.

Yes it is unfortunate, there are many starseeds on the this planet with the gift such as yours, but they get dragged down into the low vibrations. Society puts them there.

Save me, heal me, feed me, on and on it goes. When in reality, it is within themselves.

October 31st - All Hallows Eve

Soul Mission

After I parked, this weird guy showed up and parked right next to me. He gave me the creeps, so I left and found a new spot. I'm having a hard time relaxing because I feel like he might show up there. This kind of thing happens often...sexual deviants hanging around the lake. Not long ago a guy pulled his car in next to me and was masturbating while looking over at me.

Why are so many sexual deviants also drawn to this place?

There is a high vibration here and it excites them. The only time that they feel a higher vibration is during sexual orgasm, which is a time they can release energy.

So they feel the energy and they don't really know what to do with it?

Correct, they immediately reach for their sexual organs. Not only because of the high vibration of the energy, but also because of need to release it.

It's very foggy and the clouds are rolling over the water. I am reminded of the first time in the beginning, when I saw you walking in the water.

You are on a mission.

Isn't everyone on a mission?

Not necessarily. Those who are may not find it, or remember. Just as in nature the flowers scatter seeds to the wind, but they do not all take.

The creator spirit sends many starseeds to the Earth and other planets as well. But not all will take root or align with their mission. Others are here just for the experience, others for healing of relationships and karma...more of a personal journey than a mission. You signed up for a mission, and have wondered in and out of it ongoing.

The mission is to bring awareness. As you are aware, your early childhood and upbringing groomed you to be accessible and relatable - meat and potatoes. Now you can explain things in a way that people can understand and relate to.

* The reference to my upbringing is about my family and the bar that they owned. My mother would push me out into the crowd and say, "go talk to the customers." Being an introvert, this did not come naturally to me. But I see now that learning to talk to people, and be social was a great gift that has served me throughout my life.

* The meat and potatoes reference is from when I was working the psychic fairs. I prided myself in talking in a way that was easy to understand. A friend who did the same would call it a "meat and potatoes" reading.

So what am I to relate today?

The veil is lifting. Just as the clouds are lifting, so it is the veil of humanity. The walk into darkness is nearly is coming to an end. Humans are ready to reach beyond being a slave race.

Slave to money, slave to power, slave to worry, slave to slavers, slave to poverty, slave to energy vampires. The enslavement of the human psyche, the enslavement of the bodies and spirit, has been the prevalent environment for eons.

It started with those who came here to mine gold and other environmental things that are no longer available. Your Grand Canyon is one area that was mined to extinction of a certain mineral. Minerals that can be utilized in other worlds. As humans began to grow in their knowledge, they began enslaving one another as they saw the creator beings doing. When the Earth was usurped of the valuable minerals, the creator beings moved on.

The humans who were left created hierarchies of power, and the pursuit of power and dominance became the over-ruling vibration.

There has been a collaborative push to bring the Earth back from the dark ages into the light for a very long time by human time measurements. Christ was one who came forward, and many other followed. The Earth's energy is so steeped in fear that it has been difficult for those of the light to shine. Many were persecuted and others just gave up and hid their light away.

Little by little progress is being made. More are more are answering their soul mission. Many who came before had their mission picked up and twisted by religions, and other seeking power and control. The Christ message was not about the martyrdom, but more about the human race and it's potential.

John 14:12 King James Version (KJV)
2 Verily, verily, I say unto you, He that believeth on me, the works that I do shall he do also; and greater works than these shall he do; because I go unto my Father.

·

January 10th 2020

Lunar Eclipse, Saturn Pluto

Conjunction

The Purging of Dionysus.

*I am not certain what this meant. Dionysus was the son of Zeus and the God of Wine. His Roman name was Bacchus and the Greeks held a six day festival in his honor every spring. There are some accounts of Dionysus being banished (purged?) because his mother was mortal. But stories are varied. *Later I would learn that the festival of Dionysus happens every year in March, which is when the Coronavirus hit.*

A look back in time. We are cycling toward the great unfolding, the great awakening, as we have said before. Long before man walked the earth, there was a covenant of the stars in this system and beyond to sustain life and provide a place for those to flourish and grow.

She has suffered at the hands of man, but she maintains her connection to her bretherin, her sister planets and stars. She is fulfilling her commitment and her place in the greater plan. She moves in a different time space reality, as we do.

Is it the same as yours?

Not exactly, there are many. We are in a closer
time space to her than to yours, but there are
many in between and beyond. Just as you
experience time differently in your human reality.
If excited, things move quickly, while in a state
of boredom, they move very slow. It is all relative,
but still there are constraints of sorts.

A span of vibratory rate that you work with and
stay within a certain range of motion. We are in a
range that is much thicker and slower than yours,
and your mother earth is even slower yet.

I'm noticing the birds on the water.

Just as the water birds can skim the top of the
water to pull out a fish. They butt up against
another time space yet they do not enter
completely, for they would perish. They cannot
function in that world. They must stay in their
world, or their lane, for the most part, as do most
of earth's creatures.

February 3rd 2020

Sparkles

It was really sunny and warm, close to 60 degrees which is unusual for this time of year. I am seeing sparkling on the pages of the notebook.

What is this?

An extension of the ions from the water, Energetic extensions to aid in the healing process.

A portal? Or like Star Trek or what happened with Johnny?

* When I was a teen, a friend (Johnny) died and came to me. At the time it reminded me of the teleportation device from Star Trek - "Beam me up Scotty."

Not exactly, more like an awareness of what is always there. The higher dimensional awareness of what always walks beside you. An opening of dimensional fabric, a glimpse into what is already there.

Tell me more about you and your history.

We are ancient by your standards of measuring time, and we walk with the earth. We have a sort of soul contract with her, and other Terra beings. We walk with her, we observe, we protect, we honor, we elevate, and we aid in carrying out her soul plan.

Kind of like spirit guides or guardian angels to humans?

Somewhat, but we oversee the Terrras, and there is no ego. Your earth is well aware of our presence as we walk along side her on her journey. We guard and protect her while she is incarnate in this delicate condition. We have been with her from the beginning and we will be with her until the end of her incarnation. Just as your spirit guides are with you for your entire incarnation. So in that way it is similar to your guides, but in other ways it is not.

As to the term Terra beings?

What you would call planets. Each is an incarnate being who has a life time, as you have a life time in your human body. All Terra are living out a Karmic cycle that is far more expansive than you can imagine from your point of view as a human.

So some of you are of the earth and some of the water?

Yes like different races of people. We are cousins, we have evolved over time. We inhabit the space and adapt accordingly.

Are your bodies 3D?

No. We touch upon the 3D, but we are not as your physical bodies are. We are part of the environment in which we reside. The Forest, the water, the desert, the swamps or mudlands.

People do catch glimpses of us and read it in different ways: Monsters, Faeries, their imaginations. It varies from each individual. How much fear they are feeling at the time.

Are you in a higher realm?

We are of the earth plane, but not in the way you understand it. We are karmically connected to her, but took on this mission voluntarily. We are bound to her for the duration and have no regrets about it.

So what about the other planets you serve?

Yes that is our call. Some are more watery, some more forested, but all are on a similar path as your earth mother. Our kind and their kind are bound in a sacred pact. We have been incarnation together for eons, and will continue to do so.

I am seeing visions of forest and trees.

Yes we are more connected with the trees than with humans. Trees are of a closer timeline to us than you are. If left undisturbed trees can live for thousands of years, much longer than the human body.

Why are human lives so short in comparison?

It is quite an ordeal to incarnate as humans. So much trauma and emotions. Envy, greed, strife, hurt, abandonment does not exist, we do not have those experiences. We do not fight each other or have emotional excitements. We know why we're here and do what we came to do without all the additional emotional traumas, the ups and downs that you experience. We are calm and steady, never wavering, moving forward on our journey and enjoying the ride, the experience. Knowing that we are in line with our divine purpose.

February 18th 2020

The Tipping Point

There is a feeling that us coming from the earth,
knowing that something is changing. The people
try to busy themselves with this and that to
distract themselves from the overwhelming feeling
that something is coming. Something they signed
up to be a part of upon incarnating. They get
caught up in the trap of wanting to fit in and be
noticed.

Right now it is not popular place to be. They fear
ridicule and rejection, and they are not wrong.
Ridicule and rejection are part of it, but that will
not always be the case.The more people speak
their truth, then more will start to speak out.

The earth is speaking to us all, and we are part
of her so we cannot completely shut it out. Though
most are trying, the world is so loud as to not hear
her call. Just as one might try and ignore a
physical symptom, until it gets so loud it cannot
be ignored anymore.

That is where human consciousness is right now at this juncture in time. We are at a tipping point where too many are speaking out to be ignored anymore.

Feb 19th 2020

Ultra Man

Tell me more about you and where you come from. The first guys I saw the water that were like Ultra man.

Yes Ultra man creators tuned into the same thing. We inhabit many of your world's waterways. We charge the particals and ions. It is a two-way street, an energy exchange. The water feeds us and we feed it.

There are also energy vortexes in that part of the world, but it is kept under wraps. Pyramids, underground crystals, such as your geode. They are carefully guarded, but some can be seen from your sattellites.

Like google earth?

Yes and others that the majority do not have access to.

So there is a connection between this area and Asia?

Everything is connected, but yes there is a similarity due to the proximity to the large crystal. They tend to stay near the source.

There are others too, on the very tips of the earth (poles). It is easier to go undetected there becasue of the sparce population. And also in the oceans, where there are no land masses nearby. Both the Pacific and Atlantic have major populations, but are seldom seen or sensed by humans.

Where do you come from?

We do not all come from the same "planet" in the way you think of it. Just as all humanoid beings do not reside only on earth, but are seeded alll over this galaxy and beyond.

Most of our origin sanctums have disappeared long ago. Because our life span is so long, as long as a planet or longer, our origin place no longer exists. We have no wish to go back there, but instead keep moving forward.

We come from different places. The water beings come from places consisting mostly of water. Others come from places with dense vegetation, much like you jungles. So we took those characteristics in our physical visual representations. But really we do not have a 3D physical body as you do.

We appear as pure energy in this dimension. We have also picked up startdust along the way, which sort of stuck to our form. We are a representation of where we have been, our travels along the way.

Kind of like how humans get tattoos to represent life experiences.

Yes, or scars on the physical body. It clings to our aura.

Like a parasite?

No, more like a beautiful reflection of where we've been.

What can I call you? *While I didn't get a solid answer, the first thing that came to mind was "Earthmates" Then I also got "Guardians." Then later in the day while washing dishes I got "Travelers." The words Eonowak or Eonowah also came through, as well as Timewalker.

I almost felt that Timewalker may have been referring to me. I've always wanted to know my Native American Spirit name. Although I have picked them up for other people from time to time, I could never get it for myself. Perhaps Timewalkers are what they are, and maybe I am one too?

At any rate, I'm not sure what to call them, or if they even have a name in human terms. Perhaps something more concrete will be revealed to me at some point, but I'm not going to continue to press the point right now.

March 1st, 2020

Terra Beings

Tell me more about the Terra Beings.

They come from another galaxy far from here.
They came through a portal, or kind of worm hole
to enter this dimension or time line. They are
traveling, and while doing so they are unraveling
and reconnecting interdimensional fabric. Kind
of like synapses in the brain...making new
connections and adding flavor to the soup...or
like your jammming with music. Each player brings
an element or energetic input to the piece, as it
becomes part of the whole. Each contributes their
part, adding to the expansion and beauty.

*the image I'm being shown is these swimming
creatures...tadpole like things...swimming
through thick gelatinous like material with
sparkling energy coming off of it and going into
the surrounding material. All the while cutting
new pathways and leaving bits of itself in the
medium (water/gel)*

Yes like the first beings you saw wading in the
water, an energy exchange is taking place.
Each charging the other with their contact
with one another.

Humans do this also with the atmosphere surrounding their energetic field or aura as you call it. It is expanding and connecting with the surrounding environment.

This is universal truth, although occuring in very different environments. This energy exchange and partical mutations are always taking place.

Like the law of attractions?

Yes to a degree. Like attracts like. But there is also a combining factor, and with this comes a completely new energy...a combination of both.

Like giving birth to a child? Mother and father DNA/energy combines to create something new.

Yes in a way, creation is always taking place, not just in a solid form such as a child exactly. The creation changes from one moment to the next, from one millisecond to the next...it's ever changing.

*visual - I see a person walking along with sparkling particles surrounding them. Something like those lava lamps with glitter in them.

While I'm usually relaxed after a session, I was completely zonked out after this one. I was uncertain if I'd be able to drive home. It made me uneasy, and wonder if I am being drained by this. Within the next couple days I saw a few people talking about being really tired and drained, and that it was because of an energietic upgrade that was happeneing. So maybe that's what was going on for me as well.

March 9th, 2020 - Full moon in Virgo

Intergalactic Waystation

Today I decided to go to a different spot away from the city, but still on the lake. The vibration was much higher there, and I could barely get the car parked before the energy started coming through.

As I pulled up old brown leaves are blowing everywhere. There was an accumulation piled up against the fence so they couldn't get out to the lake.

In this time of renewal (spring) the old must be carried away and released. If not released, it can be stuck, like old energy and the old leaves stuck on the fence.

The old leaves are not without use, they are the fertilizer in which new growth can take place. Earth is in a continual state of renewal. You build upon what came before. And because you are in it's atmosphere, that is what humankind has done over and over again. Build up, tear down. Great civilizations have risen and fell due to the lust for greed and power. As long as this pattern continues, earth cannot ascend.

There has been a massive influx of souls who are coming to help elevate the vibration and break the long standing cycle, so that earth can break free into another dimension and join her sisters and brothers who came before her.

She has been held back for a long while. Rather than destroy this civilization and start again, as has been the practice for eons. The universal collective has agreed to try another way. That is why so many souls are incarnating. Like a vehicle that is stuck in the mud or snow. Many people coming forward to push and get unstuck so progress can be made.

The purpose of this (lesson or session) is to open your hearts and minds to the possibility of what many might call heaven on earth. Humans are capable of so much more than they are currently able to express. There are dimensions and higher states of expression, as you yourself have experienced. But for the most part is fleeting. Only for a brief moment is the connection made and then broken. Humanity can experience more and more of this glorious bliss and co-creating connection with the divine. As more and more souls join together and push forward, the entire planet can be released like the car stuck in the mud.

Journeymen. We are on a journey with your beloved mother. We will be with her as long as it takes for it is all part of the natural order. We are cheering her on, we are proud of her, and offer encouragement. For she has much to teach us all on her cosmic journey. Like a child riding a bike, looking back to make sure the parents are still hanging on by their side. She looks to us to be there, to hold her up if need be, and support her on her journey. We are not her parent however we are soulmates in a soul contract with her, and we are excited to see her through.

What about the Lake Erie Aliens?

Yes, the area has been a portal for many years, as discussed before.

The geode as you call it sends a signal that is picked up from "outer space" as you would call it. It is a beacon for space travelers to find their way, not unlike your light houses. It is also a transmitter, transmitting data information to neighboring star systems.

What about alien sightings?

Yes, many come through here. There is an entry below that leads to a waystation of sorts. The salt deposits that you mine serves as a protective barrier surrounding the entire structure.

What goes on there?

Many things, it is a waystation for intergalactic travelers.

There are multiple uses for this particular spot. Energy is gathered and stored here. Scientific studies are conducted to develop new technologies from the organic materials available here. Science research, storage areas, there is much activity. Not unlike your NASA station above the ground nearby.

Are there other places like this?

Not exactly like this one. But yes there are many all around the world. Each has a different purpose, and are located in different landscapes with varied natural materials.

At this time I was shown a vision of inside the place and also it's location related to the other deeper lake (either lake Huron or lake Michigan) There were windows looking out at the deeper lakes water very far down in the depth of the earth.

There were fish and other sea creatures swimming out side of the windows. I quickly drew a crude picture of what I saw below.

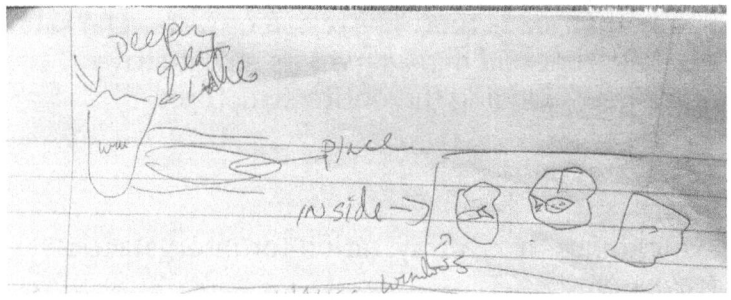

The sea creatures are very aware of our presence and come to visit often.

Again I asked for their name or what I should call them. And still I got no clear answer. It's as if it's not that important to them, and the names they are throwing out are more like suggestions rather than an answer to the question. Kinda like, "how do like this one?" lol The names I got this time were: The Wise Ones or the Ones Who Came Before Time.

March 13th 2020 - Friday the 13th

Glitch in the Matrix

I arrived at the lake to get settled in to start the download process. A red car pulled in the lot with the distorted thumping vibrating bass going on. I thought I was going to have to move to another spot, but he just did a lap around the parking lot and left. A few minutes later a different red car pulled in with radio blaring and did the same thing.

I've been experiencing these repeating scenes lately, like a glitch in the Matrix. About a week before I was driving behind a red car (red again) who was stuck behind a white box truck driving really slow. I decided to cut down a side street to get around them. About a block down the side street I was stuck behind a different red car behind a different white box truck. It blew my mind alright, and I said out loud, "must be a glitch in the Matrix."

Is that a real thing? A glitch in the Matrix?

Yes it can be, it can be a sign of jumping time lines. You are jumping time lines continuously and don't even notice it.

Can we do it voluntarily?

Yes, a good way to jump or reset yourself is to go to sleep. Every time you wake from sleeping you have a fresh perspective. You have been communing with you higher self and guides.

Like how a sports event will have a break or time out to regroup before heading back to the field. You are always in touch with your higher guidance helping you to align with a higher vibration, or better choice in any given moment.

Why were these repeating patterns happening with red cars?

To show you that pushing does no good. Red is the color of aggression. Aggressively driving and trying to push got you nowhere. And then today instead of leaving you just waited and let it pass. And they did pass. This too shall pass.

Yes it all will pass and be merely a blink of an eye when all is said and done. Pushing is not the answer. Allowing, flowing, as the flow of traffic. Sometimes things aren't moving as quickly as you would like. There could be a myriad of reasons why. It is not for you to know or push against. Just relax and enjoy the ride!

The lake is pretty choppy and it reminds me of the turbulence that the coronavirus is causing right now.

Message for all:
We are all ascending and in doing so we must
release all the stored energy of trauma, regret,
and disdain. It is stuck in our collective auras and
must be purged so that we can move forward on
this journey of a lifetime.

For as we ascend into the higher vibrational rate,
these energies and beliefs have no place there.
As we are being made aware of our conscious and
unconscious fears. They bubble to the surface
because it is time for them to go. This causes fear
in many. Still trying to control. Stay in control
of themselves, maintain control over others. It
is fruitless to struggle and only makes the process
much more painful than it needs to be. Let it pass
freely with as little interference as possible.

This is the natural way. Nature doesn't fight against
the seasons. The leaves on the trees die in the fall
and renew in the spring. It is the natural order.
Trying to hold it at bay is an enormous waste of
energy.

Rejoice in the changes for it is ever occurring.
Do not feed into the collective fear. Instead be
the beacon of light that you came here to be, that
we all came here to be. That you all have within
you as part of the divine order.

April 4th 2020 (444)

Coronavirus Quarantine

I arrived early in the morning trying to get some time in before all the people showed up. There was a steady stream of people coming and going, all seemed to be stressed and bewildered by the circumstances we found ourselves in.

I started out asking if I should continue to write the book, or just start putting the messages out on Youtube.

Your book is just a memory of a certain time space perspective created in the constructs of humanity.

Message for all:
Simmer down, simmer down, simmer down,
here and now, here and now, here and now

This is a time of peace, of much needed withdrawal. It is a grounding of the past lives to unite all aspects of our soul. Gather the scattered energy and return to center. We are gathering our belongings so that we may move on to the next phase of human existence. The next chapter of human growth potential.

It is wise to take this time to gather all the strands of time, so as to move forward as we were always meant to do.

I was seeing visions of many golden strands moving around in all directions, flowing, moving. Then they were all coming together into one strand. It reminded me of fiber optics.

I was having a hard time concentrating/tuning in because the birds were making so much noise. Squawking loudly, like in a frenzy.

Yes they are in a frenzy, just as the human population is in a frenzy.

Next a poem or lyrics came through:

They cry for the simple
For the ones who cannot
For the children in darkness
For the light of the dawn

For the good, and the evil
The weak, and the strong
The peaceful, and war like
Who's kingdoms are gone

They scream from their towers
While waving their fists
Their world is dissolving
Like fog in the mist

Farewell mighty strangers
You struggle for naught
As more awaken
you'll all be forgot

After I finished writing out that poem the birds settled down and were quiet. It was as if these words voiced what they were trying to say, or sing out.

Look beyond the birds. The weather is perfectly still. The sun is shining, yet they were in a frenzy. This is a metaphor for the what's occurring at this time.

The earth walkers (humans) are in a state of alarm. Fighting for supplies, at odds with each other, and yet the world goes on. Calmly, smoothly, like the water.

When they stop all the squawking, they can get in step with this beautiful serene day. This moment in your time is just that - a moment. There is beauty and serenity happening throughout the cosmos. This moment is less than a day, less than a minute in your soul's journey and the journey of your beloved earth.

Take time to notice the beauty, the serenity, the ultimate calm knowing that everything is getting back on track. Turn off the noise and squawking. Tune into the inner peace of knowing that you are exactly where you are meant to be at this moment, as are we all. The movement of the tides is the movement of the world.

April 18th 2020

Creativity

Tell me about the creative process.

Creativity is a most beautiful gift to mankind.
It is a reflection of other worlds that touch upon
this one in moments of divine inspiration. It is the
doorway to other worldly presence. It can bring
peace, express rage, or great passion through the
creative one. Those who partake are opening to
the great gift that is available while here.

*Are there different spirits or muses for different
types of creative expressions?*

Individuals may connect with a different coduit,
but all comes from source. These muses you speak
of are messengers, gate keepers who open the
door and allow the greater perspective to shine
through. Perceptions that otherwise might not be
seen through human eyes.

What about music?

Music is a form of divine intelligence. It is ever present in the cosmos. You may catch a stream and follow it for a time. There are multitudes of streams, infinite in number.

During this transmission I saw a vision of multicolored glowing strings flowing in every direction. Almost like sped up footage of a super highway.

Yes it is true. Energy travels through the sound like your highway systems. Moving faster than the speed of light.

It is instantaneous by your standards. There is no beginning and no end. It is ever flowing, ever present, ever expanding, ever loving, spiritual presence. It moves to and fro, expanding on different aspects of itself.

Like musicians jamming share energy?

Yes but on a much higher level. What you experience while playing music with others is but a minute particle of what exists in higher dimensions. A closer analogy might be how cells or microorganisms multiply when viewed through a microscope. As above, so below. Creative expression elevates the spirit, which makes it easier to connect with other worldly dimensional realities.

April 20th 2020

Worlds Colliding

A foot in this world and the next.
A time and space vortex or crossover.
Worlds are colliding, moving and melding.

Be still and allow divine matter to constitute
in this time of transition. New worlds are being
raised as others fall. There is no peril in it my
dear, we are all in it. As you rise, so do we.
As you ascend, we all progress.

Do not fight against those who resist, just keep
leading the way with love, presence, joy, in
exciting anticipation of what lies ahead. There
is always more. Expansion is neverending,
always present.

The robin bobs for his worms, enjoying the beauty
of the day. Nature has no fear of the future, no
disaster mind set. You are part of the natural
world in this body. Follow their lead, be in flow
with nature and spirit as all are one. Turn your
thoughts to love. Be the observer of all the beauty
this life has to offer.

April 24th 2020

The Great Awakening

This is the season when everything comes to life.
The birds feather their nest, the plants and
animals who have been dormant are coming back
to life to begin again, a time of renewal. And so it
goes with the earth. We are coming back to life
from a dormant stage that has lasted many
thousands of years by your time. Many thousands
of years by your time, but only a short distance in
the evolution of the planet.

The collective is waking from a great sleep, hence
the great awakening. Your earth has been in the
great sleep longer than your recorded history.
Longer than the current age of mankind.

As the collective wipes the dust from their eyes,
they began to see the bigger picture. It has all
been an illusion. To see beyond the illusion you
must first admit that you are not alone. This can
be a comfort to some, and distressing to others.
Not alone in the sense of the other races of man
that inhabit the universe, but also not alone in the
sense of your spiritual nature. There are many who
still believe that this earth life is all there is, and
they will cease to exist beyond this.

There are still more who believe if they can control everything, then they will be safe. Safe from what? Safe from their limited beliefs? Safe in the stone walls that surround them? Cut off from any real connection to the true form of life that is abundant on this planet and the universe at large.

When you awaken from your daily sleep, it is good to spend a quiet moment or two acclimating your soul to the new environment. The same is true for this time of mankind.

Those who push and try to force their will will have a harder time and a less pleasant experience during the awakening. Slow gentle movement, allow for acclamation to the new environment you will find yourself in. Open your eyes and greet the day! It is a beautiful place to be if you allow and are present in your awareness. It is a time of joy, not sorrow. A time of love, not fear. A time of attunement to the higher vibratory essence that is melding into your 3D reality, never to be the same again.

You are coming to the apex of mankind's journey out of the darkness. Out of the shackles of limiting belief systems that have held you back for so long. Lead the way through example, through simple things. For many are in fear and baby steps are required. Those who have not been on the path are in a state of shock and fear. They have built the reality on what can only be seen right in front of them.

Again we say lead by example. Not through righteous indignation, for we are all part of the whole, none greater than the other. All are formed through a foundation of love, and through love we can ascend. Calmly go about your soul's work and others will sense your peace. Peace is what's needed. This is the beginning of the new era which has been foretold through the ages. By walking peacefully into the new dawn, you set the tone for the new day. Peace, peace, peace, peace, peace, peace, peace, peace...

It is a universal message that has been broadcasting for some time now. More than a hip slogan from a bygone era, but a universal message for the masses.

April 27th, 2020

Pareidolia

What about the faces seen in wood and other objects? I was thinking it could be because the veil is thin and they are souls from another dimension.

The faces are real. They are there always, not necessarily of higher dimensions. Many are spirits who are still hanging around, playing little tricks through manipulating physical objects. They are not of a higher order, rather earthbound tricksters playing childlike games.

While they were talking I got an image children sticking their tongue out and saying -nah nah - nah nah nah.

Message for All:

You are of this world and you are in a 3D body, but you are part of many other worlds simultaneously.

My vision was of light strips reaching out in different directions, connecting to other worlds. Arched like very thin rainbow beans.

If you are true to yourself then the truth can come through. We are all teaching in multidimensional realities, as are you.

This earth body is but a fragment of who you really are and what you're capable of. Elevate and connect to the higher aspects of your source while still staying grounded is the in the earth plane, that is the message.

Create heaven on Earth by connecting all parts of yourself with your earthly focus. The Earth branch of your soul is the furthest removed from the source. You are just beginning to realize how vast you really are. Awake from your sleep. As you do so, others can follow. Show what is possible by living it, you can make miracles happen.

Miracles only seem miraculous to those who dwell in the darkness, cut off from their source their true essence. You can create miracles upon miracles by extending your beliefs and remembering who and what you are.

As your energy expands and consciousness grows, you can create a reality beyond your wildest dreams from this vantage point.

You are part of a much bigger coalition that is operating on many levels, many dimensional frequencies. YOU ARE NOT ALONE!
You are not alone in your pursuits to raise the consciousness of earth kind, and you are not alone in your soul journey to this planet.

There are others scattered throughout the globe on similar missions. It is preordained, thought out and planned. Though not all will remember.

The image in my mind was of throwing seeds to the wind and some landing in the dirt to take root and grow.

You are well on your way, yet there is much more to come. Much more to learn, much more to teach, much more to show. As we continue our work with you more doors will open, and more eyes will see. This is the tip of the iceberg, but is an important milestone nonetheless. Many beliefs will be shattered as we continue this work. All that you already know is but a grain of sand in the vast ocean of knowledge we wish to impart. There is much more to come. Too much too soon could feel like a tidal wave. Gentle waves are best for now.

May 8th, 2020

Adventure of a Lifetime

The waters were very rough and the waves were breaking on the rocks when I arrived.

Yes the waters are rough, but we are planted firmly on solid ground. We do not have to venture out into the rough waters. Instead we can observe the turbulence while standing safely on solid ground. Be the observer, be of it, but not in it. For this too shall pass, and a new day is around the corner.

One does not stand here and look out at the crashing waves and say, "this is the state of the water forever." We know the water is different day by day. We do not fear that the water will be crashing and violent forever. We know that it will settle down and there will be more sunny days ahead.

Everything is transient, everything is growing, moving, changing. It is the continual state of being. The waves do not stop because you wish them to, they go through their motions. It is not good or bad, righteous or evil, it just is.

If we do not become immersed in it, it cannot harm us, and we can see the beauty in it. The beautiful chaos, changing from moment to moment.

Just like the birds gliding above, riding the waves. They do not let the turbulence deter them. Rather they use it to their advantage. They dance with it, and use it to propel them upwards and onward. Never looking back, only forward to the next adventure, the **adventure of a lifetime**!

Just then a red car pulled up next to me with the thumping base. I asked - why do they come to this peaceful place and make noise?

They're on the verge of an awakening but are still fighting to stay asleep, like the people on social media. Clutching, clinging to their perceptions of reality. All the while feeling the pull of their soul to connect with their own higher guidance and soul mission.

It is a plight that many are struggling with at this time. What they were taught, is what is. All is unfolding right in front of them. They turn up the noise and an effort to drown out the voice from within, the voice of the natural world. The noise makes them feel safe and secure because it is what they know. It keeps them isolated in the 3D illusion.

They come here at this time because your energy is vibrating high and they are attracted to it, and to this place which is also vibrates high. The waves are not deterred by their relentless pounding, nor are the birds, and you don't have to be either.

Finally I couldn't take it anymore. I started the car and moved to another spot. "I guess I'm not there yet," I joked.

Perhaps not, but you could be. Be like the birds, be like the sea. Emulate nature for it is all there to see right before you. The wind seems wild with abandon but it is merely doing its job. It is blowing in a new vibration, a new current. Let the current carry you, be one with it. It is part of you, and you of it. There is no separation. It is an illusion set up in the constructs of your 3D world, your 3D existence, your 3D experience. It can take you to great heights if you will allow it to. That is what you came here to do, what you all have come here here to do.

Release resistance and allow the flow of oneness to carry you forward like the birds. Not looking back, but only forwards. That is where creation lies, in the present moment of existence, in the forward movement of the tides, in the ever-present existence of universal thought and mind.

You build monuments to your grief and wonder why there is so much sorrow. These emotions are useful in the moment but are not for the long term. Each "other" knows the part they were meant to play, and they played it well, in perfect time during their existence in your reality.

There are no regrets, no forlorn, only continual growth and movement towards a better tomorrow created in the ever-evolving now.

I threw some bread pieces out for the birds before leaving. Usually the seagulls come flying down in an aggressive mob, fighting over it the bread.

This time I waited there for quite a while and they were only sparrows, and then a couple of Robin showed up. They were joyfully enjoying the bread and seemed quite happy to share peacefully.

The seagulls were flying overhead and flew right past. Not even seeing the bread, even after the other smaller birds were enjoying the feast.

I felt like it meant that the people who are caught in aggression like the seagulls, who are loud and obnoxious, trying to overpower others, would not be able to see or hear what I was offering. My offerings, whether bread or messages, were for the peaceful - like the sparrows. And for those who are singing songs of joy - like the robins.

May 11th, 2020

Water

I want to ask about water, not just here at the lake. In relationship to psychic insights. Why do so many people get downloads in the shower, or while washing dishes, or doing laundry?

Water is a conductor yes, a conduit a medium in which contact can be made. It is a life blood of this planet and others, but not all.

Water can rinse you clean and clear resistance. It is known by your scientist to be a conductor of electrical currents, but it is a conductor of much more. Even electricity is much more than your current understandings allows for. Water is the fuel of the human body, it is continually moving through your body, and the body of your great mother in her streams and rivers. When a river runs dry the surrounding land turns dry and barren. It withers and appears to die. Without water your human body would cease to thrive.

I understand that, but how does it serve as a conduit of energy in the form of downloads in the shower, or while doing dishes or laundry?

It is a conduit that is true, but it is has a lot to do with the state of mind you find yourself in, hence the term mindless work. It is the combination of turning off the mind, and the proximity to the water, it is two fold.

So what about the planets where water isn't the criteria for life to exist? It's always bothered me that water is the measurement for which we determine whether a planet can sustain life or not.

There are so many, more than you can count. You have visited some of them that is why you are so adamant about it. Some are gaseous, that would be probably the closest to your earth bodies. Instead of water, they "run" on gases that would not allow your human body to survive. Many of these inert gases your current scientists have not discovered.

Because they don't exist here?

No, they do exist in this system but have not yet been discovered by Earth walkers of this era.

So how many other eras have there been?

Thousands, much more than your geologists even know of. Their monuments have long ago turned to dust. There will be no physical remnants of them, but they were here nonetheless.

Earth has been a habitat for life for billions of years by your measurement of time. She continually hosts incarnates who wish to learn and aid her in her soul's journey. Incarnates of your era are not the most advanced or smartest to have resided here, not by far. You are in the beginning or intermediate phase of development. Still waging war and power struggles. There is much room for growth in advancement.

Tell me more about the other advanced eras like Atlantis.

Know there were others who were far beyond what Atlantis achieved. They fled while Earth was going through a rejuvenation. Off planet, to Arcturus.

I got a visual image of Earth turning brown instead of green and blue. It reminded me of dirt being turned over in a garden. it seemed to be coming from the inside churning outward. Is that what happens every time?

No, each time is different. You know the story of the great flood. Their scientists knew of this coming change and fled the planet. Sometimes it would be fire, sometimes it would turn electrical.

With each of their descriptions a visual image accompanied it. The Earth as a giant fireball, the Earth with electrical lightning bolt type of things crackling all over, interconnected, almost like the ley lines on the Earth.

Yes that was the origin of the Earth's lay lines energetic grid that still remains today. Some of the inhabitants were able to escape to other planets or other dimensions through dimensional portals that existed at that time. Some were not so lucky, and lived through the trauma of perishing. All the while Earth continues on her journey, never wavering, always on course with her divine destiny!

What you are describing sounds like the Superman story, the author grew up in this area.

The story is as old as time and many resonate with it, hence it's popularity. Yes it was his soul story, and he was remembering another time from his soul memory.

Know that this is not a rare occurrence in the cosmos. Planets evolve and revive themselves all the time. The story has played out in many different universes and time-space realities. It is not unique, instead much more common than you know.

The reason of your mission is not to bring that information forward. Although it is of interest to you and other beings on this earth walk at this time.

Your mission is to be a beacon, a guiding light for the masses who are still in the dark. Just like the lighthouse you gaze upon during these transmissions. They are a symbol of your soul mission or purpose in this life.

The levels of consciousness you are able to access are increasing with each session as your awareness expands and your vibration is elevated.

Thank you for today's session, anything for me personally today?

You are awakening to the sound of your heart. Your ship has left the port and is journeying into the unknown. We will be with you every step of the way on this journey, and you are never alone.

June 4th, 2020

Onward and Upwards

I was trying to find a spot. There's lots of bugs and people. Some people said they saw a snake so I moved. Summer is here and lots of people and activity, despite the disease. The lake is very peaceful.

A wave of potential for all is upon the land. Those who choose to use this momentum will ride high and advance. Those who do not will fall, only to rise again and again. There is no shame or judgment, for each is on their own path. There is always a path not taken, but opportunities will arise again and again.

Humanity as a whole is poised for the great awakening at this most opportune time in human evolution. It is not only at this brief moment, it may last years by your Earth time. There is no immediate limit or rush, each moves at the their own pace. There are those who like you, that would race ahead but feel the weight of the mass. The mass of 3D reality, the mass of the masses of incarnated souls who have not awakened, and may not awaken in this incarnation.

Worry not about what they are doing, or not doing. It is not your concern. Continue to focus on your own expansion and progress. Continue to clear and release, continue to ground in the higher dimensional realities. This message is true for many more than you realize, many more than you can count.

Huge waves of people are awakening but all fall back then move forward again. This is the Earthly condition. The important thing is to keep moving forward again.

Onward and upwards.

Yes onward and upwards. Forging a trail that others may follow, or not. There are many who resonate with your message, who have had a similar Earth experience as yours. So they can relate to your struggle, and follow your path. There are many more who do not, and that is okay.

There are many teachers awakening all over the globe from many walks of life. You are one who has answered the call. Others were called and have not responded to that call, and that is okay too.

Many seeds have been scattered to the wind, not all will flower. There is no love loss for those who do not. As the species or messages are propagated, the species or work lives on. That is all that matters. It is true in all forms of procreation on this planet. Thousands of sperms but only some will take root.

Thousands of seeds from the dandelion. Nature seeds more than is needed in every instance so that the beauty lives on.

June 8th, 2020

Listen to the Children

I went to a different spot today. A lakeside park that is very family-oriented with lots of activities and kids. A red tail hawk flew over my head when I first arrived. An auspicious omen, as the hawk is a spirit messenger. Black Archduke butterflies were fluttering all about as I made my way to a sunny bench overlooking the lake. The calm lake is dotted with boaters enjoying the beautiful day. Summer is in full swing! Dispite all the activity around me, it was not distruptive at all. An afternoon of magical synchronicities ensued.

The pool of life is forever renewing. More souls incarnating to keep the momentum going. Keep elevating the vibration so as not to fall back. There is a collective incarnation or baby boom happening, as millions of souls are wanting to be part of this great ascension process. They are fresh from the other side ready to elevate consciousness as a whole, before varying degrees of conditioning can take hold. They are carrying the energy of pure intention and aiding in the awakening of the masses.

By pure energetic infusion of higher dimensional wavelengths, these souls are coming en mass to aid Earth and the humans who reside on Earth to open up to their cosmic plan and detach from the past traditions and practices that have weighed the Earth dwellers down for ages.

This is of utmost importance on their and your collective soul mission. Elevating consciousness is paramount in creating the changes you seek.

As more awaken to this vibration, the rest will take care of itself. There is no need to fight for a cause that is beholden to another. As the light grows the darkness fades. Dark cannot exist in the light, it's that simple.

Spread light, spread love, listen to the children, their knowledge is vast. They are the stewards of the new Earth that is being created at this time space of your being. Be of beautiful mind, spirit, and heart.

Just then two black Archduke butterflies were dancing and twirling together right in front of me. One was black with golden yellow markings, and the other was black with blue and white markings. Butterflies have been dancing around the whole time I've been writing, and continue to do so as I'm writing now. They are enjoying the flowering clover that surrounds me on the bench. Just then a couple of spiders join me on the bench, and I gently brush them off.

As I was writing about the children incarnating, two small children ran by and said, "let's play capture the grown-ups." I laughed out loud because it was so in-sync with what the guides were saying.

Allow the energy of these children to take the lead. To "capture the grown ups" vibration of control and denial, and open to their childlike nature, long forgotten.

An elderly man was walking his dog and the dog was aggressively barking at every child they came upon. As they approached a nearby toddler boy, the dog started barking at him, and the toddler barked right back. I laughed again and thought - good for him!

The dog is in line with the owner's energy and senses the new humans taking over.

What about the dancing butterflies?

It is the dance of love, the dance of joy, the dance of forgiveness. An infusion of their auric field, and yours as well. They feel your expanded state as you commune with the higher vibrations, and they are attracted to it.

All life is interconnected for the largest to the smallest. We all operate in the soup of resonance that we all share. Vibrational ecstasy is what is unfolding around you.

Feel it, experience it, relish in it. Let it feed your soul and elevate your existence.

As I'm writing various birds are suddenly flying in circles over my head. A few feet away from me a red wing blackbird perched on a lamp post is singing out it's song loud and clear. Perhaps they feel it too. I can't help but notice the color black repeating. The black bird calling to me, and the black butterflies all around. Then just as I'm writing this, a woman passes by walking a black dog.

Is there meaning to this?

Black is the void where creation is taking place. It is void of all color and light, yet it is powerful place of creation. Paint your world with the colors of life. You have a clean slate, like the blackboard that has been erased. Write your story, write it new, write it now. Use all the colors in the rainbow, there is no such thing as too much.

You are at the peak of creativity, allow your highest dreams to come true. There is no limits, no restraints, you are creating the new world starting now, today, everyday. Realize your heart's desires. Find the hidden treasures hiding in plain sight.

June 18th, 2020

Multidimensional Portals

Is there any info that we haven't heard from other teachers? Maybe more about the different life forms like the guardians who walk with the planet, or Inner Earth, underground or unexplored places?

There are many unexplored places, but only by your modern day society. There have been times on Earth when these places were common knowledge amongst the Earth's inhabitants. They are only unknown by this era of human inhabitants.

Many of the entrances are in areas of little or no human population, but some are in plain sight. There are multidimensional portals that are accessed by frequencies, rather than a lock and key as it might be imagined.

Some are in areas of the world where strict government control is enacted, even punishable by death. The powers that be in those regions want to stay in control.

They are presenting the illusion of absolute power as if there is nothing higher, so the inhabitants continue to obey.

I was getting visions of thick jungle and forested areas, grown over pyramids hidden in the jungles, possibly Asia.

Yes in the region you call Asia and other areas as well. The locals are well aware of the comings and goings of these multidimensional beings. Most would not speak of it publicly in fear of death or torture.

Why don't they just come forth and overthrow the government?

This is not our place. We do not overthrow or operate with brute force, as many of your fables would have you believe.

When they were saying fables I was getting visions of movies an TV.

It is up to you to find your way. We do not forcibly interfere with your collective. We simply offer guidance to those who seek it, like yourself.

What about inner earth, or the place that was described right here under lake Erie?

They do exist. Some are long abandoned, or so it would seem. There are multiple realities happening all at once and occupying the same space. The lower vibrationary humans are unaware of the higher dimensional beings also in the same space.

Like ghosts and humans in the same house?

Yes that is another example of two different life forms inhabiting the same physical space. Often not aware of one another. What we are talking about however is a much higher vibrational field than your earthbound human spirits or ghosts.

A closer comparison might be your human relationships to insects. You know there are ants dwelling below the ant hill, but you are not affected by their presence, as they are very small by your standards. So you carry on with your daily life coexisting in the same space, aware of their presence but unaffected by it.

Higher dimensional beings are coming and going continuously from your plane of existence, yet you are mostly unaware. As an ant would not be aware of your comings and goings, as it is not relative to the ant's life. So it is with our interactions with the masses.

Can you make yourselves invisible?

Invisible? Yes, but not in the way that you think of it. We are simply in another vibratory plane, or dimension. It is all happening simultaneously, separate but at the same time. It is everything and nothing at all.

It all exists in the ever unfolding universal continuum.

You are dipping your toe into the subtle energetic frequencies, different from your own. You have been doing it for years. It is very subtle, not as abrupt as many would believe. It is fluid, gelatinous, there are no distinct lanes or sharp edges. Always in motion, transformative, in and out of multiple realities. It is seamless and natural.

When you incarnate into 3D reality you are indoctrinated into the grand illusion of this existence. Many rules and regulations to keep you from realizing your expanded consciousness that resides within your human body. You are taught that there is only one reality, and you need to adhere to. This is all changing, and it is disrupting the very core of your collective existence. There are many who cannot step outside of this belief system and are striking out an anger and rage.

It is best not to join in. Just as we do not fight against or overthrow, neither should you. Maintain the higher energy as much as possible.

Commune was nature, relish in peace, that is the way. War does not create peace, war creates more war. There is, and will be, more unrest as people's realities come undone. Hold space for peace, that is the highest calling at this time. Be of peace, be in peace, facilitate peace.

All will awaken in their own time. Shine a light. Light the way so they may cross the bridge into the new Earth world. Be a beacon, a guide, a calming influence to counteract the fear. That is the highest calling at this time.

June 24th, 2020

Shopping for DNA

I have been getting a vision of female walking through some sort of organic tunnel (for lack of a better term) She is pushing a shopping cart, and I have this sense that she is shopping for DNA.

Shopping for DNA, do we do that?

Yes, as you advance and and gain knowledge you can pick and choose.

Did I?

Yes, most definitely. There were certain skills and talents that you wished to embody and they were present within these genetic lines.

Such as?

Music, art, also the ability to open up to the higher dimensions. It is present on both sides of your family tree but is not much talked about.

What about my daughters, or my grandchildren?

Yes they have chosen too. They have a soul purpose to realize, and the genetic material within your DNA has ample resonance with what they need.

Does everybody choose?

Most do, to some extent. Others are thrust into a body without much thought at all. They may have karmic ties to their parents or others in their human group.

In most cases they are just starting out on their earthly souljourn and don't really know what they need. They haven't established any particular patterns as of yet. Some come from incarnations of less developed creatures so it is best for them not to take on too much.

Just getting their feet wet eh?

Yes, just seeing what it's like to be in a human body and experience Earth life. They don't have a strong of a soul mission as others.

So the more advanced souls had these early lifetimes experiences as well?

Yes, perhaps experience soul is better terms than advanced. Advanced implies superiority and none is superior to another.

Did I have those types of lives too?

Yes, in a very primitive time. What you might call caveman. You have seen some of these.

Memories were flashing in my mind's eye. First was from years ago. A friend of mine was getting into healing. She called it "running energy." I volunteered to let her practice on me.

She had me lay on a table, and as she began the process, I got a vision of what seemed to be a past life together.

In the vision we were cavemen type creatures. She was some sort of healer or something in that life as well. She motioned for me to come into the cave where she was doing her healings.

The second vision was flashes of the many lifetimes I experienced as warriors. Some very primitive and barbaric.

Yes, and on other planets as well. Not all incarnate on Earth exclusively. You did not, as you know. There are a myriad of schools that one might attend while developing their soul growth.

It seems to me that some of the non-human incarnations I've seen myself in, were more advanced or experienced.

Yes, you have incarnated in higher dimensional realities than Earth, much higher.

You volunteered to come at this time to help the Earth Mother ascend, as have many souls who are here in this time space reality.

Have I incurred more karma in this life while being human, with human relationships?

Yes, but the work you are doing can lift you out of this. It is never too late to start your soul's work.

*As they were talking I was seeing scales being balanced out.

I've been in and out my entire life, but now I feel I'm finally really in it. I won't be trying to be "normal" again.

Yes, we agree you should not be deterred again. As we continue to work with you, you will continue to progress and elevate consciousness for yourself and others. This is your path, your true soul calling.

I've sensed for a while that I was no longer speaking with the Earth Guardians, so I asked them again - "who are you?"

Some would say the voice of god, and others who are in fear might say the devil. We are a higher dimensional collective, sent here to elevate the Earth's song.

Are you the same ones I initially talked to? The Earth Guardians?

No, they were just a facilitator to connect with us. It was easier for you to connect with them first, then we could come through and make a connection. They are still available for you to communicate with if you desire. But it is no longer necessary, as we have a direct connection now.

Are you Pleiadian or Arcturian? What is your home planet?

We are beyond incarnating at this point, we are not physical. Some have had incarnations in *Algonquin? *Dynasty? Most are outside of the realm of your human recognition. Now we have extended beyond that dimension.

I wasn't quite sure what they said..it sounded like "Algonquin." The next day I tried looking it up. Although there were no constellation by that name, there were Native American tribes.

The Algonquin were made up of several tribes who resided around the Great Lakes region. (which is were I go to do the channeling) Upon looking into their legends, I found a couple of interesting stories of interactions with star people.

There is the story of the Great Fisher. He was a magical warrior who brought summer to the lands then ascended into the sky, becoming the Big Dipper.

Then there is the story of Algon. A great hunter who fell in love with a beautiful star woman who descended from the sky in a giant willow basket.

Do you assist me when I'm doing readings?

Sometimes we dip in, but most of the time it is your spirit guides who have been helping you all along. You have seen some of them. We come through for the transmissions for humanity, that is our purpose.

When they said I have seen some of them, a particular female guide flashed in my minds eye. Years ago when I was working the psychic fairs, I got a drawing from a spirit guide artist. I always admired her work and wanted to get a drawing from her. When she completed the drawing it looked like a picture of me. I was so disappointed, as I had seen her do such beautiful ethereal drawings for other people.

A few years later I was reading at a coffee shop and I started getting a repeating vision. A female who loked quite a bit like me. She was ushering in other souls or perhaps spirit guides of the people I was to read that night. Almost serving as a spiritual recepitonist of sorts. I saw the vision of her performing this task on several occasions, and concluded that she was a helper for me while doing the readings. It also made sense that the spirit guide artist picked up on this particular guide, as the drawing was done at the pyschic fair where I was doing readings.

June 26th, 2020

The Voyage

I was wanting to get some clarification about what they said the last time about their origins.

What were you saying in the last session about Algonquin? Is that connection to the Native America tribes?

Yes, the tribal people have not lost their connection to higher spiritual knowledge and their teachings hold much wisdom.

You were referring to where you came from, a galaxy or dynasty?

It is not documented by your astronomer scientists. It is long forgotten from your perspective. Do not trouble yourself with where we came from, it matters not. We ourselves are removed from that existence. We do not cling to our origins, we are ever expanding and evolving, that is the way. Look forward, not back.

We humans have a saying - If you don't learn from history then you are bound to repeat it. lol

There is some value in that. But the idea is to keep moving forward.

Those who are stuck in traditions are impeded by that way of thought and being. While continually looking back you cannot fully move forward. Like the boat that has set sail. Eventually you will lose sight of the shore or base from which you came.

That is the purpose of the voyage. We all are on a voyage of our own choosing. Enjoy it, marvel in it, absorb the experience. Feel into it fully and marvel at the wondrousness of it all.

Is there a message for all today, maybe something new that we haven't covered yet?

The message is simple. Keep loving, keep healing, keep purging. By raising your vibration everything improves. More happiness, more enjoyment of this miraculous journey. Raising the vibration of the planet and those on it should be the primary focus of all who are seeking.

Pick and choose wisely where you focus your attention. Some that you care about deeply may not be ready to awaken at this juncture. Do not scold them or berate them. Just love them, that is all there is to do. Sending loving vibrations will do more to change the world than any amount of convincing or converting. That is not the purpose of life.

Lead by example, raising your vibrations will spread, not unlike the virus so many are concerned about at this moment.

Spread love, it is more contagious than any virus. The power of love trumps all.

Create an atmosphere of love wherever you go whatever you're doing. Simple deeds can be more powerful than grand gestures. Take pleasure in the simple things. Perform daily tasks with care. Be kind to those less fortunate, less educated, less enlightened. We all are on our own path to enlightenment.

The path can be beautiful if you allow it to be. Be the beauty, be thankful for the gifts that are all around you. Make time for gratitude, make time for appreciation, make time for love.

July 2nd 2020

Multidimensional Selves

So what is this book about? Is there an overall theme?

The first is about your experience, making our connection. Many would be interested in how you came to this point, as they are striving for the same. There are clues for others to follow from your journey of discovery. Then as we go forward topics will advance, some more complex, some simple truths.

What is the message for today?

That your world is changing, changing at a rate that is incomprehensible to the human psyche.

It is like the undercurrent or undertow.
From the surface the water looks very calm,
yet beneath there is a riptide, pulling you
towards a new reality. Some would stay on the
shore, while others will dive into the deep end
unaware of the current that can take them away.

Eventually all will succumb to the flow, for it is inevitable.

If you are still on the shore, dip your toe in the water. If you have left the shore, keep moving forward, not looking back. The future is bright, it is on the horizon.

Humanity as a collective is being pulled forward, being called by your future selves from the highest possible outcome.

Feel the pull, connect to it, hear their call, answer back. Keep the channel open. You may eventually lose sight or feel as if you've lost the connection, but you have not. It is still there.

Even those caught in the lowest of vibrations are still connected. No one is lost, you simply forget from time to time that you are a part of the divine. This connection is everlasting, unsevered, unwavering. You are part of the divine cosmos and your potential is infinite.

As they were speaking, I was seeing the face of an old man whose face is superimposed over stars in space.

Call out to it, as it's always calling out to you. The denser the vibration, the more difficult it is for the signal to penetrate the density. That is why again we say elevate your consciousness whenever possible. Keep that idea in the forefront of your thoughts and mind.

Allow the divine into your very being without putting up roadblocks and excuses. You came here to help change the world.

Open up to your full potential. Most on Earth are only living a fraction of their potential. This is not said to make you feel like a failure, but instead as encouragement. By elevating humanity, you can begin to enter into the bigger conversation, the larger collective.

We are here to help you on your journey. Remove obstacles and limits, they are man-made constraints put in place by the laws of man. There is a higher law that is universal. The law of one, the law of abundance, the law of LOVE!!! Love is the only truth that matters in your reality. It is the gift of light and the greatest tool for expansion.

Love in the face of adversity, love in the face of fear, loving the present moment, love is the way, the light, the answer, love is all.

Some would mistake love as sacrifice. What you might call giving your power away. This is not the highest expression of love that we are speaking of. Sacrificing yourself to another is shutting down your own light. That is not universal love. That is succumbing to the lower vibrational rate. Agreeing to be less so another can have more is not love.

Universal love is shining so brightly that the lower vibration cannot be sustained. It is shined right out of existence. By shining brighter you expand your vibration to those around you.

Yes you will fall from time to time, that is the human condition. Forgive yourself, love yourself. You are a divine being of light sent here en mass to aid in the revolution of this planet. Exciting times indeed! Feel into the excitement, not the fear. Both are elevated experiences. Each may choose which way to utilize the energy.

this is something I figured out years ago when playing in bands. If I ever felt a little nervous, I would turn the energy into excitement, and yes they are a similar vibe for sure.

Am I part of a higher collective?

Yes you are of our group. That is why we can connect to you.

Like a soul contract?

Yes in a way, there was a per-life agreement. but everything is not set in stone. it is ever-changing, flexible, a part of you is consciously creating it all the time.

When I sleep?

Yes, you returned to us when your body sleeps. But it is not as if you are in your body when you wake and with us when you sleep.

You are always with us, only a small portion of your true self is emerged in the human body at any time. You are with us right now as your human body is taking down the dictation.

What about that onion head girl I saw? Is that me too?

Yes she is who you consider to be your best form or true self.

* A few years back I kept seeing a vision a creature. She had a human body and was wearing some sort of a robe, Her head was shaped like an onion or bulb. Her skin was white with pastel translucent colors in it. At one point I saw her in my hallway with something like a clip board. That's when it occurred to me that she was part of me.

Was she gathering up various parts of my soul? Like a soul retrieval?

Not exactly, she is like a supervisor of sorts. Gathering is not the right term. More like keeping track of all the pieces of your soul existing on various timelines. Although she looks strange to you from your human eyes, you see her as the most beautiful from your souls perspective. The true you for lack of a better term.

* While their talking I'm thinking of cousin Marilyn from the Munster's TV show.

Although she would be considered beautiful by our standards, the Munster family always remarked who homely she was.

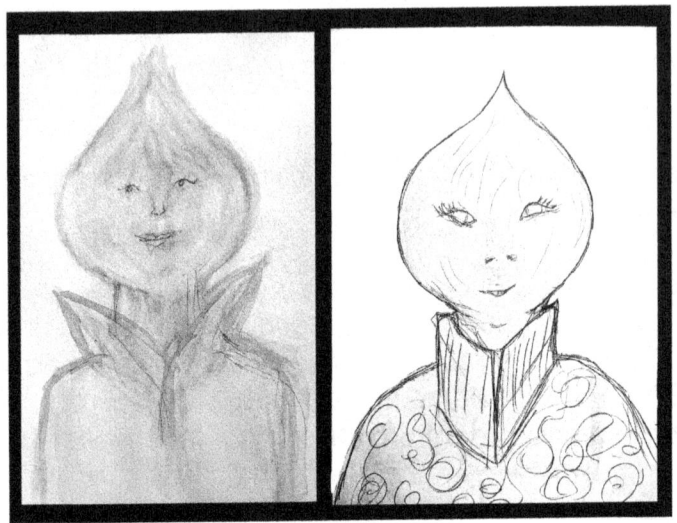

Pictured above are two different attempts to capture her likeness. The image on the left is a watercolor done right after I first saw her. The second is a drawing done in 2020. Neither is a very good likeness. The guides told me that I'm trying to make her too pretty by earth standards.

The onion head woman was not the only alien like creature I'd seen in my life. As a child I saw myself as a blue skinned creature. I was tall with very long fingers, more fingers than a human would have. I remember asking my mom what happened to my other finger.

What about all the visions of the blue fingers and such as a kid?

Yes that is part of you also. You came from that dimensional experience just prior to this Earth experience.

There were teachings that were imparted upon you that you could call upon in this lifetime.

What sort of teachings?

How to navigate the Earth's plane, and other things that are much more subtle regarding using a 3D body and mind to connect to alternative realities. The visions you saw as a child were like a test signal to make sure that it took, and the channel was open.

What about my mom and other family members?

They all chose to be part of it. None of them were able to progress as far as you have at this juncture in time. But they will continue to do their work, many in other dimensional realities.

What about my mom when I told her about the blue beings and the extra finger?

On a soul level she knew exactly what you were talking about. But she was not ready to face it at that moment.

As you know, she wanted to be normal and fit in more than anything. She still did a lot of good in her life to help many.

My mom did help many people who came into the bar over the years.

Olga on the other hand made great strides. not only because of the hardship she endured.

But because of the density of the era in which she incarnated. With each generation the energy becomes lighter and lighter. as the veil becomes thinner and thinner.

* Olga was my maternal grandmother and earliest spiritual teacher. After her mother died, her father had to put the kids in an orphanage. This was a fairly common practice at that time as there was no social services. She suffered really harsh conditions there, and also as a young woman.

July 11th 2020

Hybrids

* It seem that asking specific questions is boding well for these sessions. So I am pulling out many of my personal spiritual experinces for more clarification.

* One such occurrence concerns a man who has since crossed over. I did not really know him in this life, but started getting visions of he and I being together as a couple. It was not a fantasy, as I wouldn't even be thinking of him and these visons would just come on. In one particularly intense vision, I saw our teenage (at that time) daughter. It seemed so real, I knew her name and age, and when she looked at me, we knew eachother. For the purpose of this book I will refer to the man as CC.

CC and me, is that real?

As real as can be.

So we are connected?

Oh yes, through many dimensions.

But not in this one?

No, the connection was missed, and missed again.

What about me and the daughter that I saw?

She is real, she is one of a few.

One of a few?

Children who are not present in this reality.

So what other children are there?

The son that everyone predicted, he's true too.

* Back when I worked the psychic fairs, it was common for readers to do exchanges for one another. I was told on multiple occasions about this son I would have, but it never happened.

And others that you have no idea of. It is too far removed from your current reality.

The two we have mentioned have brushed up close enough to feel or sense them. The others have not. You saw the girl because of your deep connection to the man, as she was your offspring, and a great love as well.

It sounds like that would be one of my best lives, and this one is one of the worst?

This line is one of the more difficult. but that has pushed you to reach the state.

In another reoccuring vision, I see myself standing in front of a huge glass window. It is just before dawn and I'm looking out at the sunrise, I believe I am in Hawaii. I am in a state of perfect contentment as I gaze out at the sunrise.
I turn to my right where a man lies still sleeping in the bed. He is laying on his stomach and I can't see his face, but I know that we are in love.

What about the vision of Hawaii, with the man in my bed? Is that the same timeline as CC?

It is an offshoot of that. Each line has many possible offshoots from the initial storyline, as you might call it.

Can I still achieve that? Be in that space with that man?

Yes it is possible, that space at least. You never see the man because he is inconsequential and could be filled by any number of beings. But the "space" and the state of being can absolutely be achieved.

Another reoccuring vision I've had is of me sitting in a screening room watching the animated TV show or film of my Green Glen Characters. The Green Glen is a children's book and animation that I created.

*In the vision I start crying when I see them on screen. The other people in the room laugh and say something like "there she goes again."
It's as if they know me, and I guess I have been crying throughout the production. I also cry in this reality everytime I see the vision.*

An interesting side note: Prior to getting this vision, I always drew and animated the Green Glen Gang flat, in 2D. In the vision they appear as a 3D annimation.

What about the other vision of the Green Glen in the screening room?

That is real as well.

I mean can that be achieved?

Something similar can occur, but that particular sequence of events is far from where you are now, and unlikely.

* The next question has quite a back story. To truly explain it I have to go back quite a ways.

When I gave birth to my twin daughters, the Governor of our state was campaigning and was going to stop at the hospital I was at. They told me about it and brought my babies in the room with me, and another new mother into the room as well. The plan was to talk to both of us, as our stories were very different.

Whle we were waiting for the Governor to arrive we started talking. She told me her story of multiple miscarriages, and how her premie baby was in the other room fighting for it's life.

There I was, not even trying to get pregnant and I had two healthy babies. I felt sad for her and almost wanted to give her one of my babies. Of course I didn't, but I felt her pain.

When the Governor and his entourage arrived they swooped into the room accompanied by reporters and photographers. They crowded into the room and surrounded me and my babies. I couldn't even see the other woman, and nobody even talked to her or noticed her. Meanwhile we were on the local news, and had our picture in the paper, and she wasn't even mentioned.

That experience always stuck wih me, and years later I heard about egg donation. I was serious about doing it because I thought it was so unfair that someone who wanted kids so badly couldn't have them, and then there's me - fertile Mirtile, not even trying and ends up with two!

After reading the literature I did not end up doing it because it required a lot of drugs and hormone injections. But if the drugs weren't required, I would have donated my eggs for sure.

Many years after that I got a glimpse of these adult beings that I felt very strongly were my *children. Their environment looked something like the fairy kingdom as depicted in the Lord of the Rings movies. They were doing artwork and showed it to me, although I can't recall what it looked like now.*

I wondered if wanting to donate my eggs if no drugs were involved all those years ago, that I was consenting for this to occur.

What about the hybrid children I saw?

Yes you agreed, not only in your human consciousness but as a soul agreement as well. The whole scene in the hospital was key. It was made to make an impact on you.

Are they fairy or ET hybrid?

They have your genetic material as well as others. You could name them Fairy or ET, neither is 100% correct. The other genetic material is not of the current Earth human, so ET could be correct.

Is there any more to say on this topic that I haven't touched upon?

What you call hybrids is happening all the time, with all sorts of species, from many different planets and dimensions. They happen off-world because most of the time the different dimensional vibrations or reality cannot coexist in one or the other.

So a third environment must be found or created where they can coexist.

It is not "evil" or wrong, it simply is, and has been since the dawn of time. The current humans walking the Earth are not the original model as your scientists already know. We are always creating, all of us, even you creating new realities continually.

Many of us who created these vehicles or bodies also incarnate into them. We are anxious to take them for a test ride, and offer data for improvements and upgrades. Just as a mechanic is excited to take a car or motorcycle that they have designed or built for a ride. Or your Wright brothers, who built many prototypes of their flying machine. Each design improving on the last.

So am I one of those who has designed bodies?

You have been, but now you are concentrating on different areas. Lifting consciousness, and creativity mainly.

So these hybrid children, am I in contact with them other than the fleeting glimpse I saw?

Yes they move in and out of your range of vibration, as they have their own soul missions. Your genetic material has given them gifts they need to further them on their journey and they are grateful to you for it.

But they are not of the earth plane and must continue on their own soul path.

Will we be united again after this incarnation?

You are always connected, but they have their own path to travel. There are others who are closer to you in your soul group.

* Another thing I was curious about is when birds do what I call "The Happy Dance." It's when then fly right in front of you or in the car flapping their wings in front of the windshield. I feel like they are telling me something good is on the way!

What about the birds doing the happy dance?

Yes you are always in touch with nature. Your oversoul will often speak to you through other earthly creatures. Other creatures of Earth are more connected to source and have not been programmed for the most part. They are clear channels always tuned in, always open. Some of your domestic animals are more caught up in your frequencies in an attempt to communicate with their captors. But none are as disconnected as humans.

When you are strongly focused in your 3D mind, we send animals to bring messages that you maybe unable to receive it in this state. it is very common though many do not even notice these messages and signs put in their path through nature.

The animals are happy to cooperate as it takes nothing away from them. They are not put out by it or angered, as some humans would be. They're happy to be of service and are unencumbered.

July 13th 2020

Rh Negative

* I put together a list of questions and had them
ready for the day's session. Although Rh negative
was on my list, it was not at the top of the list.
I wasn't planning on asking about it today, but RH
negative kept coming through on my drive there,
so I decided I best ask about it.

So what about the RH negative blood?

Yes it is pure the blood of the elders as was
intended for the species. There have been many
mutations and turnabouts through the ages,
changes and developments.

So what was so urgent that you wanted to tell me?

Not urgent, just a topic in which we would like to
address.

You know there have been many models of human
put upon the planet. Some have survived and
others have faded away or been wiped out
intentionally. The pure ones (Rh negative) have
not been infiltrated with the hominoid bloodlines,

and there were safeguards put in place to keep
this line pure.

*If a mother is RH negative, her body will create
anitbodies to attack and destroy an RH positive
baby in her womb.*

The Hominoid types of early humans were slaves,
bred to be controlled easily and not think for
themselves. Centuries of breeding and
manipulations strengthen these traits, as humans
in your time may breed dogs to accelerate desired
traits.

Those of pure eventually brought them (hominoids)
into their homes to perform domestic tasks, and
eventually care for their children. As those traits
were cultivated, the hominoid humans grew
emotionally and in intelligence.

This evolved over many thousands of years by your
time measurements, and the gap between the two
races grew smaller. As time passed they were
indistinguishable, one from the other.

As happens in these circumstances, people fell in
love and wanted to procreate. Yours is not the first
civilization to discover a workaround to the
safeguard. So interbreeding took place. Although
the technology is different, it is as today where
intervention was needed to bypass the safeguard.

Those civilizations have came and went, and until
recently a technology has arose to allow pures to

give birth to non-pure children, as was the case with you.

So what is the difference?

The pures have a higher sense of perception and can easily access the higher dimensional realities and frequencies. They're more aware of the worlds in which they came and have less animal like tendencies.

* As if to illustrate their point, as I was writing, a couple pulled up next to me in the car. They were arguing really bad and the man was very animalistic and he kept telling her to "shut the fuck up." They were arguing right outside of my window to the point that I had to move.

But don't we all even the pures have non-pure traits in our makeup?

Yes to a degree, but there are many factors at work, it is not just blood. Some can be explained through your current scientific language. Your scientists do not understand there are many paths of discovery and manipulation. As we have said the fail safe bypass used today is not the same as those used in other civilizations, yet they achieve the same result. That is allow pures and non-pures to procreate.

The same is true with all branches of science and technology. Your scientists are able to travel into space by jet propulsion, and other civilizations traveled into space using different power sources.

Much of your tactics are not optimal, and are limited in their trajectory. This is true in all branches of scientific discovery including medical treatments.

You are going about it the hard way from our vantage point. Your advancement will be limited as a result. The burning of fossil fuels, the pharmaceuticals, all are limited in scope by comparison to other civilizations, including those on this planet and others.

Science has never been my forte, so why not relay the more detailed scientific info to scientists out there? Is it because they are too much in their "scientific mind?"

That is true for some, we do not attempt contact with those types. They are still of value though. They can take the information given, or the "discovery" and run with it. Their mind works in a particular way, once given the building blocks.

There are those however that can, and have received downloads of alternative means of advancements, but their ideas have been squelched time and time again.

I've heard of these stories, alternative energy, cures for diseases?

Yes they are true. Some of them are not true, though they are thrown in to make it seem all a fantasy or conspiracy. These types of things do occur in your society, many of them never reported.

So what is the solution? Can we get back on course?

Just keep raising consciousness, and awakening minds and hearts. When the world reaches the tipping point then all sorts of information that was previously suppressed will come pouring through.

July 20th 2020

2nd New Moon in Cancer

Neowise

What about this comet? Does it have any significance or message to mankind?

It is a peek into the souls of humanity. For you an omen of the transitory times you find yourself in.

There is accumulated knowledge stored in its atmosphere as it collects data along its way. You have come very far since it's last visit in some respects, and have fallen back in others.

It is collecting data from many civilizations on its journeys. It is a record keeper of sorts. You are but one stop along the way. As it moves in closer to your atmosphere, is able to connect with the soul vibration emitting from the collective. There is also data in the planet itself. Your great geode is one such place that serves to store information.

What happens to the data after it's collected? Where does it go?

To a higher consciousness, there are many such activities throughout the cosmos.

Speaking of geodes or stones, I want to ask about the crystals and stones energy. I have that amethyst that I see crystal people in. Can you tell me more about that?

Yes the stones can serve as portals. Spirits can come in and use it to speak to people, or for other purposes.

What other purposes?

To check in on the three-dimensional reality. Rocks are solid as you know but they are also crystalline. This allows for different frequencies of energy to flow through them.

So the people I was seeing in the amethyst are real?

Yes they were there to assist you, not only in doing the readings, but also as guardians and guides for you on your journey.

Do different kinds of rocks have different beings associated with them?

They are not necessarily associated with any particular being. It is all about vibration, and there are no limits to which beings can align to any particular frequency, as is demonstrated with your alignment to our frequency. Although other humans may not be able to align with it. As to your question, different type of rocks or stones hold different frequencies, so it is all relative.

What about how people assign meanings to particular rocks, like rose quartz is for love for example.

The meanings you are referring to are in the collective consciousness, however they are not exclusive to those defined meanings. We would encourage everyone to use your own discrepancy when working with stones.

What was true for another may not be true for you. You are drawn to the stone's energy that you are meant to connect with, and how it works with your particular vibration may not be true for another.

We would like to talk to you about peace. Peace is an internal state of being, not an outward expression. It is important for you to connect with inner peace in this time of transition. For peace to exist externally, it must first exist internally.

Finding moments of peace throughout the day is paramount to seeing improvements in your life and the world at large. Another term for light workers could be keepers of the peace.

The phrase from my Catholic upbringing came to mind: "peace be with you, and also with you."

Yes there is power in that phrase. Not everything in your religions are false, there are many truths. Finding peace is paramount to finding happiness.

What are some ways we can find peace?

In nature it is a bounding. Nature is always at peace, even in the face of destruction. if it is time for it to go it does not resist.

** I'm seeing visions of violent storms while they were talking about in the face of destruction.
I thought about the pig screaming on the way to it's slaughter from a video I saw, and also the tree screaming in front of my house. After hurricane Katrina the city came and cut down the tree in front of my house. It was a cool tree. There were always mourning doves gathered in it because they liked to eat the seeds from the flowers. Although a couple branches were damaged, I didn't think it had to be cut down. I thought I heard it screaming as they were sawing into it.*

What about the tree screaming in front of my house?

That was taken by mankind's intervention. It was not time for it to go. It provided shelter and food for the loving doves, and was very happy doing so. The same as with the pig. It might have lived a long and happy life if not for the intervention of mankind.

What about the family lines, family karma? Generations of impoverished and others so privileged and entitled?

Yes it is in your genetic makeup. This can be the most difficult cycle to break. Not only the cycle of poverty, but other cycles as well, such as abuse, alcoholism, ignorance, hate, there are many traits to overcome.

Is that why people incarnate into these family lines? I always thought it was karmic, like an eye for an eye. For instance if you were an alcoholic in one life, then you have to experience alcoholism in this one.

It is true that one would experience all sides of a given situation. But it is not like payback as you might view it.

Part of your reason for incarnating into a challenging family situation is because you feel you may be able to do the most good there. To break those chains and reprogram the DNA for future generations.

What about DNA upgrades from ETs?

This is true as well. But what we are speaking
of here is innate, and the best work can be done
from within the human form while incarnate. This
is one of the many challenges that are taken on
as an earth human. The karma you speak of is
multifaceted and encompasses much more
than your earthly understanding.

*What can we do to "break the chains" of our family
lineage?*

It is different in every case. You did a great service
to your line by closing the establishment that
caused so much pain for you and your
predecessors.

That does not mean that future generations cannot
slip back into that pattern, but the connection has
been weakened significantly by your actions. These
patterns aren't often broken by one individual in
one human lifetime. It is a collective effort tied
into many souls born into similar experiences.
These experiences run the gamut, and many are
not as obvious as the case in point.

** In my case, both of my grandfathers were
alcoholics, as was my father. My family owned a
bar which contributed to the situation. After my
entire family of origin died relativly young, I was
left with the bar.*

I did keep it going for several years but realized that it was draining the life out of me, and had contributed to all of my family's untimely deaths. So finally, against everyone's advise, I closed the bar for good, and have never regretted it.

July 24th 2020

Plant Spirits

Many people speak of communing with the Ayahuasca plant, and that is actually a spirit guide of sorts. Is it true with mushrooms, pot, and other hallucinogens?

Yes it is true, all plans have a spirit. You know them as the devas. Each plant spirit serves a particular function in human body and mind. The psychedelics as you call them can open a portal to alternative realities that exist alongside of your 3D perception.

There are many more psychedelics on the this planet than your current Earth walkers are unaware of. Many have been used in ancient societies then fell out of favor, being lost to humanity. Others were kept alive through tribal traditions. There are parts of your world where these plants still grow, but are ignored or unrecognized by the surrounding societies. They are seen as nuisances or pests. (weeds) And still they persist, so that one day the Earth creatures may rediscover their magic.

Haha yes! Pot has been known as "weed" for many years. What about pot in particular?

Pot, as you call it, opens up channels and relaxes barriers between Earth walkers and all that is already there. It may slow down or accelerate vibrations to align with creative energy that is always present.

Tell me more about the plant spirits, particularly of psychedelics. How did they come to be here?

They're companion spirits to Earth similar to the guardians of earlier communications. They agreed to come here and express themselves in order to aid the Earth and her inhabitants on their journey.

Do they express themselves on other planets as well?

Yes similar, but not exactly the same. it is again akin to the relationship of the different guardians. Cousins, I believe is how they termed it.

So there are "cousins" on other planets, but they express themselves in different forms according to the planets environment and flora. They have been working with the Earth for a very long time and have adapted and transformed along the way. just like how in recent years your cannabis cultivators have forged many different strains that are far removed from the originals introduced into western society.

I had to laugh because people of a certain age will remember smoking "Mex" short for Mexican. Then there was Thai stick and Colombian Gold and Sensimilla. But now there are so many varieties and it is so much stronger than in those early strains. Many of my friends say they can't even handle the pot of today.

Yes that is true. All the species of the Earth evolve, and the evolution can be sped up through outside intervention. As is the case with human evolution, as we have already discussed.

I paused to look at the water. I was mezmerized by the light of the sun reflecting off of the ripples in the water.

Ripples of water, ripples of time, ripples of consciousness. It is all in sync with divine consciousness. These ripples you see in the water are happening in the air, in the body, and the Earth. It is not easy for your human eyes to perceive, yet it is happening nonetheless.

There's more than meets the eye.

Yes much much more. Even though it is not currently possible for the Earth humans to perceive all that is happening. As you expand and elevate and connect, you will see more and more. It is always available to you, within your grasp. "Ask you shall receive." A simple truth, yet profoundly powerful in its essence.

July 29th 2020

Sea Creatures

So what about the Lake Erie Monster?

Yes it is true. It travels through from another
body of water deep below, not accessible to
man at this time. There is a passageway that
connects to these higher bodies of water, but
it is not always accessible. During certain times
it opens and creatures from the subterranean
will come to the surface.

The atmosphere is different, as it is for humans
at high altitudes. The atmosphere is different than
that which you are accustomed to, therefore one
may have difficulty breathing. The same is true for
the subterranean sea creatures. There are many
species who reside there that man has no idea of,
nor they of you, for the most part.

Where is this subterranean place?

There is a large area below these waters
(the great lakes) and they exists all over the
world. Occasionally a creature from the depths

may wander into your lakes, but ultimately they must return to whence they came.

Billions of years of evolution have conditioned them to live at great depths.

What about the Loch Ness monster? Is that the same sort of creature?

Not exactly, but their story is the same. The Loch Ness Monster is a closer relative of the dinosaurs that once roamed the Earth. The species took to the water to avoid the burning fire and destruction on the Earth's surface. Over time became adapted to living in the water exclusively.

Your "monster" is a different species. More closely related to manatees than a dinosaur. Both have developed in your vast subterranean seas that are present all over your planet.

Is there a message today for humanity?

See the boats on the horizon? See how they skim the surface gliding over the waves? They are carried by the water and it lifts them up. As it does so, it creates a very joyous experience. They are enjoying the ride. This is our message to you - enjoy the ride!!! Ride the wave above all the turmoil and strife. You will get where you're going much faster, and with greater ease than trying to tread water fighting the current. Allow the current to carry you and do the work for you.

It does not have to be so challenging, in fact it is not meant to be that way at all.

You have mastered the task of energy manipulation long long ago. It was part of your preparation prior to your descend into a human form on Earth.

Remember, connect, utilize this gift to humankind. It is there for the taking. It is present all around you. The caterpillar to the butterfly, the seed to the flower. Transformative waveforms are all about. Ready to transform this life into something so beautiful and previously unimagined. You are masters of creation!

July 31st 2020

Blue Beings

There was a huge 600ft, 12ton barge heading towards the mouth of the river when I arrived. Although the lake is used for entertainment, it is also still used as an industrial waterway. An ode to when this city rose up during the industrial revolution over 100 years ago.

The waves carry the heaviest barges to the lightest leaf, and it supports them both with ease. It does not discriminate against as to who is risen up. Even the heaviest vessels can be lifted into the light. Nothing is impossible, only your beliefs make it so.

I wanted to ask about the movie Avatar and the Nav'i. The Nav'i are so similar to the drawings and sculptures I've done in the past. When I saw that movie I thought that he and I must be remembering the same place. I've also heard stories of people crying when leaving the movie, wanting to go and live on Pandora. Have we all had past lives there, or a similar planet?

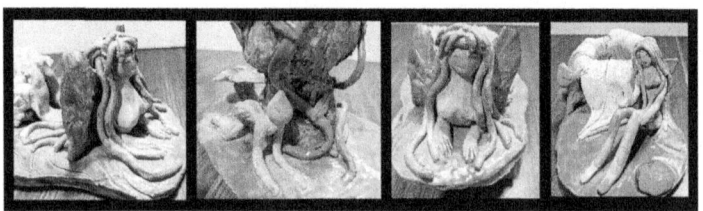

Some of my sculptures from the 1980s, all have blue skin.

There are vast legions of blue skin beings living in this and other galaxies. You have known this from your earliest years of childhood. The Nav'i as well as the beings of your art remembrances, are not exactly the same. They are two of several thousand such races scattered throughout the universe. Yes many walking the Earth now have had incarnations in these galaxies.

James Cameron's and mine seem to have a similar vibe. Connected to nature, the hair, even the headpieces they wore.

Yes there is a similar experience, but that is true throughout the expanse. As we have told you already, Earth is a low vibrational place. The majority are more evolved, and in harmony with the natural word, as we advise you often.

The two in question (Avatar and mine) are both from very peaceful societies that are in close connection to their natural environments. The third race revealed to you in your childhood (long fingers with extra digits) are scientists, geneticists, mathematicians, and other areas of studies that are beyond your earthly comprehension.

You have connections to both.

What about Hinduism, Shiva and other gods? Also the blue people that live in Appalachia - the Blue Fugates. Are they remnants from a blue alien race?

Yes there is a true genetic connection with the Blue Fugates. There were blue beings that visited ancient India as well. To support knowledge and to impart the Earth walkers of the time.

They also visited various other parts of your ancient world. There is a genetic component connected to your Asian race that is more conducive to blue interdwelling of species.

They intermingled among your Native American tribes. Those genetic markers are present in the hill people. (Blue Fugates)

As to the Nav'i, in the movie they are connected to these trees (vitraya ramunong or tree of souls). The trees are very willow-like, and I myself have always been attracted to willow trees. Since I was a child, I love to watch weeping willows blowing in the wind outside my bedroom window as I drift off to sleep. I feel a very spiritual connection to them as well.

Yes the tree holds a sacred connection on this planet and others. Eons ago the elders tried to bring samples of the sacred tree to this planet, but it could not thrive without being genetically altered. Although much different from the roobie tree, The willows still retain some of its original properties.

What properties?

It is one of many terrestrial beings that embody higher consciousness and wisdom. It is particularly beautiful, kind, and wise, and loved by many throughout the cosmos.

* I'm seeing a vision of this tree tree sparkling and emitting light and glowing. A feeling of pure love and remembrance came over me.

Yes, an energy source of pure love. The true tree of knowledge that many have sought after.

So back to different races of humans on Earth. Are they all starseeds from different planets?

Yes, and there have been many more. Some are no longer present, such as the blue people we have been speaking of.

After the last Earth cleansing that ended the dinosaurs reign, humans still alive lived in little pockets scattered throughout your world.

Through inbreeding over many thousands of years, certain genetic traits became more pronounced to adapt to their particular environment. So again very much altered from the original starseeds. Universal upgrades are continuing all the time as we have previously discussed.

August 1st 2020

Space Eye

I've always had a fascination with eyes. I would draw them constantly while growing up. Later in my teenage years I had an idea for a music video for my band. I invisioned an animation similar to Yellow Submarine. In my version we were in a spaceship, and come upon a giant eye in space. The eye opens up and we fly into it, entering another vast space.

That idea never left me. Years later I took a course in computer animation. For one of the projects I created an animation of a giant eyeball in space. As it opens up the viewer flies into the eye, again entering another universe.

In more recent years the Hubble Space Telescope has been releasing amazing photos taken in scace. The minute I saw a photo of the Helix Nebula I was blown away. It looked like a giant eye in space that I had been imagining all these years.

Does this lead to another dimension or universe as I imagined?

Yes it is a portal, and you have traveled through it, hence your remembrance of it.

Where does it lead to?

It is a doorway to another time-space. It does not lead to only one specific place, but can be dialed into various locations or realities depending on a number of factors.

Such as?

There are cycles of alignment that are factored in, just as your earthly space travelers understand. They launch their ships when Earth is in closest alignment for optimal success. This is right and true.

Another comparison within your understanding would be tuning into a radio signal. You have to be in a good location in order to dial in the frequency. The same is true with these passageways.

So how many different places can you go to through the eye?

Innumerable.

Speaking of space, some people believe that spaceships hide in the clouds. I thought that ships weren't solid matter, or could make themselves invisible.

Yes it is true that "ships" as you call them may use clouds as sort of a camouflage. Also the particles contained within them to manifest into 3D matter.

It's only a partial manifestation, but can close the vibrational gap enough to allow for greater communication and data collection through enhanced clarity.

August 4th 2020

Death Fractals

The last of my questions center around death and multiple timelines. My brother died at the young age of 35. In recent years I was getting visions of him as an older man. He was middle aged and had a grey beard. I mentioned this to my daughters, and one of them said she had been having dreams of him as an older man as well. It got me wondering if he had lived on in another timeline when he died in this one.

On a similar note, I have had multiple experiences where I mysteriously stopped my car for no reason. In each case I avoided a serious if not fatal car accident. I wondered if I myself had died on another time line, but lived on in this one.

I want to ask about multiple timelines as it relates to death. When you die do you keep on living on other timelines?

Often that is the case. as with your mother. She is having a hard time letting go as was shown to you. A strong part of her presence remains.

I hadn't even thought about this. I have dreams often about my Mom. Usually she is still at the bar that my family owned and operated for decades. The other thing I believe they were referring to was when my Mom was close to making her transition I had a vivid dream. She was sitting in the bar crying and sobbing. My deceased brother and father were on either side of her. It seemed as if they were comforting her, and trying to get her to come along with them.

Is there anything I can do?

No she will release in due time. Part of the reason is her concern for you, having left you all alone. The two of you are deeply connected, although not readily apparent in this life.

What about the visions of my brother growing older and having grey hair?

Yes there is a timeline where this is so. Souls will sometimes splinter off into different fractals in order to help others deal with their earthly lessons.

A big part of him did die at age 35. It had to, as it was becoming unsustainable. The part that lived on, that you saw in your vision, had been sober for 20 years. Thus he was able to sustain the physical form for a longer duration.

What about the near misses and the car accidents with me?

Did I die on another timeline, but I lived on this one?

Yes but it was a very small fractal that perished. Because of your attunement with higher consciousness we were able to get through and intervene. You were spared because of the importance of your soul mission and your close alignment with it. Even when you turned away from the path, you were still closely aligned with it. Your connection was kept strong through your creative pursuits. In other words you never veered so far away that you couldn't resume. Even if it seemed so in your conscious mindset.

Regarding these fractal timeline splits, is it ever 50/50?

No in most cases the majority goes in one direction. There is a small portion that explores the alternative.

My immediate questions have been covered although I'm sure there will be more. I suppose I will open up questions from others for future books. What would you like to say to wrap up the first book?

Message for All

There's a great vastness of experience out there for those willing to take a chance. You did not come here to be in fear and stay in a box.

You came here to expand your consciousness and growth in ways only available in this plane of existence. It is no small undertaking, but at the same time it is! That is the dichotomy. That is part of the duality of this experience. It is not just in the form of good vs evil, us vs them, but it is also self-imposed restrictions vs total freedom to create whatever you desire. By doing so you show others what is possible.

Money is not evil, success is not evil, there is no shame in creating great abundance and happiness in your life. Bask in it, revel in it, enjoy it to the best of your ability while you are here. Enjoy your time here, be an example of light incarnate.

As the sun rises on this new day of mankind, rejoice in its arrival. As you are all facilitators of this quest.

Even if you think you are ordinary, think again. For you are a divine spark, sent willingly to be a participant in this monumental birth experience. It is often noted by those who have experienced the birth of a child as a miraculous event. You have a front row seat to a miraculous event of grand proportion that is taking place right before your eyes!

More than that, you all are participants in this glorious event of human evolution! This is exciting news! Turn your fear into excitement, you're pain into joyous growth, your trials into wisdom.

Everyone reading this is being called to their soul mission. Each will answer in their own unique way. Listen to your soul song for answers, for there is a part of you that knows exactly what your role is to be. Do what brings you joy and fulfillment, what fills you up with love and satisfaction.

The answers are simple. there's no need for deep contemplation or struggle. Those on their path speak of time going very quickly. They may work for hours and it seems like very little time has passed. That is because they are on track with their soul mission.

It is easy to find if you have the desire. It comes from within your core being, and is not determined by the opinions and promptings of others. Only you can know what is your truth. Look within for guidance and follow the path that is uniquely for you.

Although this is the end of the first book, there will be many more to come if you allow. Your life experience has made you a valued messenger that many can relate to and understand. The intention is to take you and your readers along on a journey of discovery and growth. Now that we have established a flow of communication, there is much to relay to your listeners and readers.

We welcome questions for future transmissions as they can be a vehicle for further growth, and also aid us in gauging the rate of comprehension thus far.

Love to all! We are very happy to have made your acquaintance, and will be in touch again soon!

Made in the USA
Coppell, TX
15 April 2021

53806530R00095